the

eBay

book

UNOFFICIAL UNOFFICIAL

The website's most weird and wondrous...

Crombie Jardine
PUBLISHING LIMITED

13 Nonsuch Walk, Cheam, Surrey, SM2 7LG
www.crombiejardine.com

This edition was first published by
Crombie Jardine Publishing Limited in 2004.
1st reprint, 2005

ISBN 1-905102-19-4

Compiled by Crombie Jardine
Designed by www.mrstiffy.co.uk
Printed and bound in the United Kingdom by Clowes

Contents

Introduction

Introduction

The internet has changed the way we live today and we cannot now imagine what life would be like without it. Along with Amazon and Google, eBay has become an integral part of our daily existence.

In this book we have collected some of the strangest and funniest items that have turned up on eBay.

Marvel at the haunted painting that was put up for sale with a warning. Stand back in amazement at the sale of seeds to grow your own cows. And prepare to be shocked and repulsed at the same time by the serial killer's signed fingernails.

If you come across a story that you think should be included in a future edition of *The Little eBay Book*, please email us at: ebay@crombiejardine.com.

tasteless 'collectables'

PICK OF THE BUNCH

- Serial killer fingernails signed

- Hitler pin cushion

- Collectable old bottle with a
  dead mouse inc.

- Iraqi scud launcher bronze bar / ingot

Serial Killer Fingernails – Signed

Three of the 1970s' serial killer Roy Norris's fingernails. The nails are affixed to the back of a portion of a Christmas card and Roy signed a note to authenticate the nails, signing in full over a print of his thumb. One successful bid: $9.99!

Hitler Pin Cushion

It's not Hitler's actual pin cushion that he used when sewing buttons on his uniform, it's (described as):

> *a RARE item. [...] and the cushion where you stick the pins is his Butt.*

Minimum price requested: $1.00 only. After 9 days, 21 hours + there'd been no takers.

Collectable Old Bottle with a Dead Mouse Inc.

Marketed as a real conversation starter, this collectable was thus described by 'Coho' from Anchorage, Alaska:

Old bottle with Schenley embossed on neck and on the bottom it says federal law forbids sale or reuse of this bottle. [...] Inside is a dead mouse for character which I will leave in upon sale.

Coho has other bottles on eBay, with more being added on a regular basis.

After 1 day, 4 hours +, this one failed to have reached the reserve bid of $3.00 (+$3.20 postage and packing). No takers.

Iraqi Scud Launcher Bronze (not Silver) Bar / Ingot

Not just one, but 12 ingots were available for $9.50 (+ postage and packing) only for 8 days. These were described by 'Loinpro' as:

Operation Iraqi Freedom Iraqi Mobile Scud Missile Launcher Hitler / Hussein War Criminals "Challenge Coin / Ingot" Pure Golden – Bronze

On one side, the ingots depicted a camel
with a scud missile upright in his mouth
and an Iraqi soldier swinging a sledge
hammer at the camel's exaggerated
testicles which lay on a tree-stump.
The other side of the ingots showed
Hitler and Hussein and the wording:

War Criminals Must Pay For Their Crimes.

Each ingot measured 1.96" x 1.14".

cheeky

PICK OF THE BUNCH

- A fart in a jar
- An autographed jar of poo
- Fresh, clean urine
- Five raccoon penis bones
- Absolutely nothing
- A used handkerchief
- Annoying cat
- Empty box
- One deflated red balloon
- Creative genius
- Wedding invitation

cheeky

A Fart in a Jar

This had been on the system for 9 days, 12 hours +, but had had no takers. This item, summed up in an admirably concise way – "a jar with a fart in it" – remained at $5.00.

Autographed Jar of Poo

Maybe the fart in a jar was just too expensive... Here was an autographed jar of poo (3 turds).

After 5 days, 1 hours +, there had been 5 bids. First bid $0.25, last bid $1.00.

Fresh Clean Urine

This was described as:

> Drug and Alcohol free urine, female.
> Next day delivery, not for illigal [sic]
> purpose 8oz.

Starting bid of $100.00 requested.

After 2 days, 20 hours +, this New Yorker
had had no takers.

Raccoon Baculum (penis bones)
SET OF 5!!!

Five raccoon penis bones in mixed
sizes, which Jeff described as being
in 'good' to 'better' condition, and
professionally cleaned (not a job he'd
want, he emphasized!).

After 6 days, 4 hours +, there'd been one
bid for $5.00.

Absolutely Nothing

Nothing. At all. Wanna buy it?

Hugh Lowry, from Cobham, Surrey,
you win the prize.

The auction lasted 3 days, with (an unmet)
reserve of £15.00 (c.$22.00).

Used Handkerchief

Only one handkerchief, but it was 100% cotton and had been placed in the freezer after use, to keep it as fresh as possible.

Bidding to start at $0.99
(+ $1.50 for shipping).

After 7 days, 21 hours +, there'd been no takers.

Annoying Cat

Annoying cat from Austin, TX. In the words of the seller:

Annoying cat. Vomits constantly, coughs up hairballs 1-2 times per week, and wakes you up at 3am on a consistent basis by meowing outside your bedroom door.

Minimum bid just $0.01.
No takers after 5 days, 22 hours + .

The Empty Box my Computer Came in

'Secondshot' from Oceanside, CA, was selling the box his computer came in and - at no extra charge - the week-old paper in it.

$1.00 (+ $5.00 shipping).
Unfortunately the auction ended with no bids.

One Deflated Red Balloon!

This genuine deflated red balloon was
blown up and then deflated by the seller
'Thege765' who was asking a mere $0.01
for what he described as:

*a very rare and hard to find artifact, so
get your checks and money orders ready,
because MR. DEFLATED RED BALLOON
IS COOMIN' TO TOWN!!!... Coming to an
Ebay auction near you...*

The auction lasted 10 days, with one
bid for $0.01.

Creative Genius

Here was the chance to bid for (one page of) the amazing story-telling abilities of this 'creative genious' [sic]..! James admitted he was not 'a writer per se' but truly believed he was blessed with creativity. This is supported by his 6th-grade English teacher's assessment of his capabilities:

James, even though your spelling, grammer [sic] and punctuation are completely wrong, I found your story compelling and unexpectidly [sic] refreshing! A+ See me after class.

No bids.

Wedding invitation

In October 2004, Twinklydog was offering an unwanted ticket:

I've been invited to the wedding of a mate of mine who I used to know really well until he started going out with the girl he's going to marry. She's a dog. No really. I haven't seen them since I told her she's a dog over two years ago.

The wedding invitation was for two people and included a sit-down meal in a four star restaurant and an evening 'piss up'.

Twinklydog updated the description in response to a flood of questions about the bridesmaids and dress code, etc. Someone offered £300,000 before Twinklydog finally admitted that he was pulling the auction because he still loved

the old dog, despite what she did to me. And thanks to the Colchester Massiv's "Honk if you're Twinklydog's Dog" campaign, she got in touch this morning and we've had a good chat.

He was off to Aberdeen to try and put a stop to the wedding and marry her himself!

humans – whole

PICK OF THE BUNCH

- Grandma for sale

- A college student's life

- A slave

humans - whole

Grandma for Sale – MUST SEE!!!

Dubbed 'the auction of the century' this 100% authentic Grandma was up for grabs. Coming complete with history – born in the early 1900s, she had lived through World Wars I and II as well as the Clinton Presidency.

Grandma apparently loved cleaning house and picking up after people.

Grandma came with accessories:

* two pairs of false teeth
* one rocking chair
* a quilt
* a spare pair of clothes
* a pair of glasses.

Included was a 30-day full money-back guarantee.

After 5 days, 9 hours +, there had been 9 bids, the first bid of a paltry $10.00 had been eclipsed magnificently by an offer of $1,000,300.00.

A College Student's Life!

At first you might have read this as 'A College Student's Wife'. No, this was a whole life up for sale.

Goofydorky from Tallahassee, Florida, said you could have it: his friends, pictures, etc. All the background would be filled in for you, to avoid those tricky moments when you can't quite place someone who you so obviously should be able to.

After 5 days, 0 hours +, 8 bids had
been placed and the stakes had risen
from an initial measly offer of $100.00
to $10,100.00.

Slave

Zac, a 6-foot tall 16-year-old, self-confessed-Keanu-Reeves-look-alike could apparently clean windows, floors, dishes, clothes . . . you name it, he'd consider it. Cars were his specialty. But he thought skating was fun, too.

As long as you were a female between 16 and 25 years of age, 5 foot 9 tall, with long legs, then you could apply. In fact, you could be a blonde, brunette or a redhead.

(Unfortunately, Zac's reserve bid of
$1.00 was not met.)

humans – parts

PICK OF THE BUNCH

- Fully functional kidney for donation
- Testicle available
- Toenail clippings
- A glass eye
- Young man's virginity
- A conscience
- 11 inch white human penis
- High IQ sperm
- 20 full global sfx prosthetic human eyes

humans - parts

Fully Functional Kidney
for Donation

This perfectly healthy kidney was to be
donated in exchange for 2.5 million dollars
to a charity of the donor's choice.

After 4 days, 21 hours +, - no bids.

One Testicle Available

And here we had a seller with a wonderfully
succinct summing up of the item on offer:

one healthy testie for trade. seriously.

Bidding to start at: $500,000.00.

After 6 days, 7 hours +, no bids.

Toenail Clippings

These were not just ANY toenail clippings.
For a start they were reportedly 31 inches
long, and, in the words of the seller...

*you can use them for absolutely
nothing so buy them now.*

After 4 days, 0 hours +, there had
been no bids, so the reserve of $50.00
had not been met.

A Glass Eye

'Mojo-man' was offering the beautiful
brown glass treasure at a bargain price
of $9.99. Some people were obviously
on the look-out for this as there'd been
8 bids after only 1 day, 20 hours +.
Last bid $31.00!

N.B. Was part of set, only one available.

Young Man's Virginity

After offering his virginity to the highest bidder, 9 days, 22 hours +, later, Francis Cornworth had had 17 offers ranging from $10.00 to $10,000,000.00. Francis, going into his Senior year at High School decided to lose his virginity and use the eBay craze to see what he was worth.

Francis' mini C.V. boasted 'lead trumpet in jazz band', in the top 5% of his class, and 'a proud completer of 400 community service hours, last year alone'.

Francis thought he'd be desirable if he could only find the right woman – or man, even; he was willing to experiment.

A little P.S. asked kindly that if you were over 60 or knew that you carried an STD you need not apply.

My Conscience

*I am selling my conscience, cause
I don't want it or need it, you can have
fun with it.*

A conscience belonging to 'Krimsunx' from
Dallas, Texas, for $5.00 minimum. After 9
days, 14 hours +, no takers.

11 inch White Human Penis

With no warts or any other kinds of V.D.
On its own for reasons of 'two-timing',
it was just hanging out on ice waiting to

collect $25,000.00. After 6 days,
12 hours +, it was still there,
with no bidders.

High IQ Sperm

Background: 35 year old male, 15/16th
German, 1/16th Irish, 175 lbs, 6'2", blonde
hair, blue eyes, healthy, highly intelligent,
computer systems professional, good at
solving problems.

9 days, 16 hours +, and no-one had
offered anything, let alone the reserve
bid of $250.00.

20 Full Global Sfx Prosthetic Human Eyes

Starting bid of $250.00 (+ $8.90 postage and insurance for the set) requested for 20 sfx eyes used for the movie industry. Made of 'hardwearing polymure-resin-glass compound', the eyes were described as very 'lifelike', in a variety of colours, and measuring 26mm ('lifesize').

The auction lasted 5 days but there were no takers.

only for the gormless
and / or gullible

PICK OF THE BUNCH

- The meaning of life
- A roll of toilet paper
- Nine used toothbrushes
- Real Arkansas civil war dirt
- The sun
- Kennedy, Bisset memorial Cape Cod water
- Cow seeds
- Real, authentic NYC street dirt
- One dollar
- Genuine Glastonbury 2004 mud
- Ark of the Covenant

only for the gormless and / or gullible

The Meaning of Life

'Postmil' from North Carolina was confident s/he had the reason for our existence all sewn up and would be

*happy to share this information
with the highest bidder.*

Result: After just over a week, there had been 8 offers, between $1.00 and $3.25.

Toilet Paper

One roll of toilet paper - excellent condition - really soft too, Sauternes, Chicago, Il.

Colour and brand not specified.

$70.00. No takers after 9 days, 10 hours +.

9 of My Used Toothbrushes

For $0.50, 'Djcrookedrabies' was offering
9 of his very own toothbrushes, all used,
of differing brands (including some of
the best: Oral-B, Mentadent, Crest, and
Colgate Plus).

Shipping and handling charges within the
US all paid for.

6 days, 4 hours +,
later... no bids.

Real Arkansas Civil War Dirt
(No Reserve Yall)

Arkansas ('where the civil war was at', says 'Vallcome') war dirt, 100% guaranteed to be from the civil war area. 1lb of dirt. If needed, a certificate of authenticity could be provided, and Vallcome adds:

*also have provenance which will varrify [sic]
beyond a doubt that this is the real thing.*

In under a fortnight the auction had ended,
with two bids and a price of $2.75.

The Sun

A fantastic thought, but where would
you keep it? And you'd also have to
collect it from the centre of the universe.
These practical questions might bring

your average dreamer down to earth but 'Mischief99' seller didn't seem to think those were serious obstacles when he put 'the large ball of incredibly hot gas' up for sale for $10,000,000.00.

After 9 days, 19 hours +, ... no bids.

Kennedy, Bisset Memorial Cape Cod Water

50 vials of water from the bay in Cape Cod... These apparently contained special water:

gathered on the very day of the Kennedy, Bisset memorial at sea. These vials could even have fragments of the ashes. You never know. Own a final piece of memorabilia. These are limited [...].

After 6 days, 17 hours +, no bids.

Cow Seeds!

Grow your own cow herd with this complete
starter kit. Instructions included.
1,500 kits available, from the frozen Tundra
of North Dakota. Only $1.50 per kit,
including postage, and yet after 5 days,
22 hours +, there'd been only 2 bids?!

In the inimitable words of the seller, 'Artragious', there's so much to be gained from this purchase:

AND... when little Johnny ask's [sic] "Dad, where do Cows come from?"... Dad no longer has to say "Ask your Mother." Now you can SHOW little Johnny... "They come right from COW SEEDS, Johnny, here look!", as Dad pulls out a package of COW SEEDS! TERRIFFIC [sic], EASY TO CARRY, NOT-SEEN-ON-TV (yet!), and you can tell everyone that you got them on eBay!

Real, Authentic NYC Street Dirt

NYC dirt, sold 'as is', on the grounds
that it would make a great gift item...
The thing is, after 7 days, 15 hours +,
Jeff had had only 8 bids, resulting in a
latest bid price of $3.25...

The seller's descriptive powers play an
important role in the success of an eBay
auction, and Jeff was certainly full of ideas:

Now you can procure and own some of the same city dirt that celebrities, politicos, common thugs and industrialists have stood upon, since time immemorial. If you can't make it to the "Big Apple", at least you can have some of the "Apple" come to you! There's no telling how old this authentic NYC dirt sample is, but my guess is that what you are bidding on is at least THOUSANDS of years old!

$1.00 – One Dollar!

'Unclerampy', from New York, NY, was selling this rare item as:

> slightly used – ready for you to use!

Billed as 'actual legal tender', the minimum bid was $0.72 (+ $0.33 for shipping and handling [a stamp] within the US, more if to be sent abroad).

After 6 days, 9 hours +, one bid of $0.67 had been placed.

Genuine Glastonbury 2004 Mud

'Fresh' the morning it was put up for sale on eBay, here was your chance to own your own little piece of Glastonbury. 'Sandilav' had scraped it off the boots of his son who'd just returned from the festival.

After 3 days the bidding ended and offers had increased from £0.99 (starting bid) to £490.00!

Glastonbury 2004 Mud Framed by the Darkart

Well, the power of selling is such that 'Sandilav' got £490.00 for his fresh Glastonbury mud (see p.71) but 'Afatdogseller' only got £25.99 for his mud, framed by the darkart. And Afatdogseller was far more thorough in his description of the item:

Carefully collected from the book of the artist himself (usually a photographer), the piece of mud measures 4 cm x 5 cm and is imprinted with the symbols of the wellington boot's sole, making this piece of dried Glastonbury mud very cool. Framed and mounted in a (7 in x 7 in and 1.5 in deep) beech box frame, this is a quality piece of memorabilia ready to be hung.

Ark of the Covenant

Categorized, naturally enough, in the 'Antiques: Ancient World' section, this one generated 15 bids, the first being $29,425.21.

Here's the seller's description:

Yes, this is the Ark of the Covenant, used to contain the 10 commandments of God. A simple stone box, this was found in the back of my garage among a number of odds and ends left over from my days in the middle east. [...] Qualified buyers only. Nazis and evil people, don't even think it, this item has a history of flash burning of the eyeballs of the unpure [sic] and sending them down to hell (a product flaw, and one you must sign a release for should you be the winner bidder). [...]

'Cdibona' went on to explain that no photo
was available because every time one was
taken it just came out a blinding white.
$10,000,000.00 offered (shipping extra).

must-haves

PICK OF THE BUNCH

- Brand new Russian military patrol boat

- Used penis enlarger

- Rare shrunken head from Amazon tribe!

- Real cow skull

- Five genuine cat turds

- Pocket lint

must-haves

Brand New Russian Military Patrol Boat

'Soviet-Trader' seller was offering a comprehensive deal on this 'superb vessel': picture links, complete specifications, filed import / export documents, delivery (to Maryland), set-up and training by Russian PHD located in Washington, DC, was all included.

In fact the only thing not included seemed to be armaments.

After 20 hours, 22 mins +, the 44 bidders were only $100.00 away from the minimum bid of $85,200.000.

Used Penis Enlarger

Who cares if it's been used or not, it comes from Beverly Hills, CA, and 'is a steal at $1,000.00' according to the seller.

The auction was for a week, but with only 4 hours to go there'd been no bids. If you missed the auction, the following website was recommended ('for other exciting used products that we have for sale'): PenisEnlargers@altavista.net.

Rare Shrunken Head from Amazon Tribe!

'Foxvalley7' was selling not one shrunken head but 26. When you read the description, it was a little conflicting – were they authentic real or authentic replicas? In Foxvalley7's own words:

Authentic SHRUNKEN HEAD from the Amazon in South America. I got these from a Jivaro Indian Tribe in the Jungles of Ecuador that used

to shrink human heads, now
they make these life like replicas
out of animal skin!!! Form and hair color
varies from dark brown to gray. *GET THIS
UNIQUE ITEM WHILE YOU STILL CAN!!!*

Real Cow Skull

For $9.99 (+ postage and insurance) you
too could have had a real 'cow skull in
decent shape'.

No takers after 9 days, 5 hours +.

5 Genuine Cat Turds

'Kitty Turd', from Orlando, FL, thought these little gems ('Five individual cat turds' sold as a set for $5.00) could be used for all kinds of fun, including paperweights or dog toys.

After 6 days, 17 hours +,
there'd been no takers.

Pocket Lint

Maybe one of the secrets of selling or getting people to bid is to tell them they don't want whatever it is you're selling. 'Saminala' tried this with:

Trust me, you don't want this.

Setting a high price ($10,000,100.00 minimum) for what was, presumably, his own pocket lint – the location was given as

right hip pocket (don't even try)

– there were 4 bids, the first being
$12.00, the latest (after 3 days, 22
hours +) was $10,000,000.00… which was
$100.00 short of the minimum required.

sexy subjects

PICK OF THE BUNCH

- Act in an erotic cable TV movie

- The latex glove Rebecca Loos used in *The Farm*

- One hundred thoughts about sex

- One night with someone else's wife

sexy subjects

Hey Guys, Act in an Erotic Cable TV Movie!!!

Fellas, here was your chance to get star billing in your own erotic cable TV movie, have your name appear in the credits as 'executive producer', and get a contract entitling you to 5% of all the worldwide earnings from the finished film. Five gratis copies of the video for yourself included.

The bidding started at $5,000.00 but after 6 days, 6 hours +, there'd been no takers.

Rebecca Loos, C5 *The Farm*, Genuine Pig Glove

A brand new entry when this book was being put in hand, this was [allegedly] the latex glove that Rebecca Loos used to pleasure THAT pig on *The Farm*.

Apparently the glove was

acquired from a Wiltshire man doing his bit
for recycling, enough said!

'Dealboy' happily boasted that he did not
sell BOARing stuff!

My Next 100 Thoughts About Sex

'Lipmanaj' from Washington, DC, offered to write down his next 100 thoughts about sexual intercourse on a pretzel bag and send it. Thoughts would include things like perversity, ordinary longing and stress induced terror.

The minimum bid was set at $1.00 (and even a ball of string was acceptable as payment) but, no bids after 5 days, 19 hours +.

One Night With My Wife

'Rodreily' was offering to the highest
bidder his 23-year-old wife who was
'a little shy'. Apparently she wanted to
experiment with other men and also women
(possibly).

The couple needed 'money for a down
payment on a house'.

The young, blonde, 36C-bust college girl
was willing to be a sex slave for one night
to the highest bidder.

Minimum bid $15,000.00. After 2 days, 13

hours +, there'd been no takers.

Amazing Strap-On Breasts from Mauritius!

'Buckbean' from Chicago, IL, was offering this fascinating fashion accessory for just $9.99 (+ $4.00 shipping).

Buckbean describes the article as follows:

*11-1/2" across with attached cloth
tie-straps. Made of thin plastic (like
a Halloween mask) [not such a great
comparison, perhaps, Buckbean].
Made in the island/country of Mauritius.
Be the first one on your block to
own a pair of these! [...]*

No takers.

It's a Picture of My Butt

'Corben', the self-billed 'sexy guy from Florida' was charging a minimum of $1.25 for a picture of his butt. Not shy, Corben told people:

you know you want this.

After 2 days, 2 hours +, the bidding was at $1.00.

miscellaneous

PICK OF THE BUNCH

- New boys underwear *Star Wars* size 4

- I'm no prince but the
  girls still love me!

- *Big Brother 5* suitcase,
  pink case with wheels

- Airedale terrier 'War on Terror'
  fridge magnet

- TV presenter's banana

- Haunted painting

miscellaneous

New Boys Underwear
Star Wars Size 4

Two pairs of (new) underwear, Fruit of the Loom brand, celebrating *Star Wars Episode 1*. 100% cotton.

After 2 weeks 'Budlight' got them for $2.50 + $2.50 postage and packing.

I'm No Prince but the Girls Still Love Me!

Five watch-frogs for sale at $8.99 each (+ $4.00 shipping) and no takers after 7 months!!!

This little electronic motion-activated item offered to keep watch for you. The idea was that you'd place him somewhere obvious and, being the motion-sensor-frog he was, he would alert you – with a big "RIBBET!", of course – to anything or anyone crossing his path. He even had a built-in switch on his belly so that he could take a nap when you didn't need him to watch your pad... [geddit?]

Big Brother 5 Suitcase, Pink Case with Wheels

Here was the chance to bid for Emma's suitcase, as used and seen on the *Big Brother* programme. Emma's tag and photo were included and 25% of the money raised was to go to MENCAP.

She got an amazing response – over 500 emails, 43 bids and a total of £1,950.00 all in 10 days!

Airedale Terrier 'War on Terror' Fridge Magnet

Quite an inspired collectable, here.
For $3.99 (+ $1.85 postage and packing)
you could have been the proud owner
of one of these magnets featuring this
'adorable breed'. Professionally factory
manufactured, the picture on the front
of the magnet was of the dog sitting
in an open-topped shark-plane (it had a
nasty set of teeth). Underneath the
picture was the wording:

Airedale Terriers are...
Fighting The War on Terror.

TV Presenter's Banana

Kate Greenaway caused a bit of a stir on ITV's *Good Morning Breakfast Television* when she ate part of a banana in what can best be described as a provocative fashion... In response to a joke by her colleague Ben, she signed the fruit and here it was, up for auction on eBay – with all proceeds to go to the charity NSPCC.

After 45 bids it was sold for a grand total of £1,650.00!

Haunted Painting

Here's a little background: the painting was found discarded behind an old brewery. One day the new owner's 4-year-old daughter mentioned that the children in the painting were 'fighting' and coming into her room at night. Her father set up a motion-activated camera and, sure enough, on the third night apparently a boy was seen to leave the painting.

The artwork came with the following disclaimer:

Warning: do not bid on this painting if you are susceptible to stress related disease, faint of heart or are unfamiliar with supernatural events. By bidding on this painting you agree to release the owners of all liability in relation to the sale or any events happening after the sale that might be contributed to this painting. This painting may or may not possess supernatural powers that could impact or change your life. [...]

The auction lasted 10 days, had 30 bids and was finally sold for $1,025.00.

EBay Diary

If you are planning to put numerous items
for sale on eBay, it makes sense to keep
a diary of when you submitted goods and
when the auction ended. Then you can
check the outcome.

Use the following 4 pages to
keep a record.

EBay Diary

Item	Start date	End date	Min bid	Final bid

EBay Diary

Item	Start date	End date	Min bid	Final bid

EBay Diary

Item	Start date	End date	Min bid	Final bid

EBay Diary

Item	Start date	End date	Min bid	Final bid

Getting to the bottom of it

And last but not least... getting to the bottom of it all...

You may have thought, as you read this book, that one story stood out in your mind as the strangest item put up for sale. However, this is our pick of the bunch. It is a story of dedication and obsession so amazing that one wonders just what sort of man this could be. Let's set the scene...

A man in his 70s passes away suddenly. His son, who is clearing out the house, comes across what, on first inspection, looks like six bulky stamp albums.

On opening them he finds a lifetime's collection of gussets from ladies' panties... and not clean ones at that! His father had, since his '20s by the look of things, collected women's gussets and catalogued every conquest by cutting out the gusset and sticking it into an album. A grand total of 354 samples were carefully catalogued (each entry was accompanied by the woman's name, age and performance).

This collection could only have been for the pleasure of one man. It is not the sort of collection you could bring out at a party. We know this collector had a relationship with his son's mother and it goes without saying that he may have spotted his mother's gusset and description in the collection. What went through the son's mind at this point is anyone's guess. Obviously not much, as he decided to cash in by selling his father's collection on eBay!

This, in turn, begs all sorts of questions: Was the mother still alive? Was she aware of this obsession? And if so, was her purchasing of undergarments blighted by gusset-quality considerations?

Collecting women's underwear is a common enough pastime, but gussets constitute a truly mammoth obsession...

So the collection went on eBay and after a
week and 458 bids it reached $4,058.00:
Who says the bottom has fallen out of the
market?!

And the moral of the story is:

>   Make sure your collection is
>   something you would be proud of,
>   if found after your demise...

www.crombiejardine.com